Have You Seen Zandile? was first performed at the Market Theatre, Johannesburg from February 6 to March 8, 1986. With Gcina Mhlophe playing Zandile, Thembi Mtshali as her grandmother, mother, and friend, and Maralin Vanrenen directing, the play ran at the Market Theatre for a second season from July 1 to August 8, 1987.

Zandile was also part of the Edinburgh Festival in the Traverse Theatre from August 9 to August 29, where it won the Fringe First Award.

After the Edinburgh production, *Zandile* was produced in Basel and Zurich, Switzerland, and then in London at the Bloomsbury Theatre from September 15 – 26, 1987.

It's American premiere was presented in Chicago in 1988, with Gcina Mhlophe again playing Zandile, as well as directing. Ms. Mhlophe won Chicago's Joe Jefferson Award in 1988 for Best Actress, as well as the Sony Award in Britain.

In 1989, The Carpetbag Theatre Company of Knoxville and the University of Tennessee's Center for International Theatre Research presented *Have You Seen Zandile?* at the Theatre Project in Baltimore, and Knoxville, Tennesee. This production starred Edris Cooper as Zandile, Linda Parris-Bailey as Gogo and Lindiwe, and Adora Dupree as Zandile's mother, Lulama.

Have You Seen Zandile?

– a play originated by Gcina Mhlophe, based on
her childhood

Gcina Mhlophe
Maralin Vanrenen
Thembi Mtshali

HEINEMANN/METHUEN

Heinemann Educational Books, Inc.   **Methuen Ltd.**
361 Hanover Street   Michelin House
Portsmouth, NH 03801   81 Fulham Road
Offices and agents throughout the world   London SW1 6RB

This edition published 1990 by Heinemann Educational Books, Inc.
First edition published 1988 by Skotaville Publishers, South Africa.

All performing rights in this play are held by Market Theatre and application for any kind of performance in whole or in part should be addressed to the Market Theatre, Box 8565, Newtown, South Africa.

Library of Congress Cataloging-in-Publication Data

Mhlophe, Gcina.
    Have you seen Zandile? : a play originated by Gcina Mhlophe, based
on her childhood / Gcina Mhlophe, Maralin Vanrenen, Thembi Mtshali.
        p.   cm.
    ISBN 0-435-08600-6
    I. Vanrenen, Maralin. II. Mtshali, Thembi. III. Title.
PR9369.3.M68H38 1988
822--dc20   90-33908
                                                                CIP

Cover design by Wladislaw Finne.
Cover and frontispiece photos by Eric L. Smith ©1990.

Printed in the United States of America
10 9 8 7 6 5 4 3 2 1

To the memory of my grandmother, Gogo, who deserves praise for the storyteller in me. – Gcina Mhlophe

CONTENTS

SCENE ONE

ZANDILE AND BONGI

Zandile is heard off-stage saying goodbye to her school friends, who are going in the opposite direction. There is a lot of talking and laughing and the hubbub of taking leave.

ZANDILE: Umbonile ke lowa mfana ukuthi ushaywe kanjani esathi wenza lokuhlakanipha kwakhe kanti kade eseboniwe ... washaywa ezinqeni – vumphu vumphu! Wabaleka. Zamhleka-ke ezinye izingane. Hahahaha! Nihambe kahle ngizonibona kusasa, heyi Nomusa, ungakhohlwa phela ukuphatha is-kipping rope mina ngizoza namacryons – I'll bring my cryons ... Nomusa you promised hawu ... mpff, kanti udlala ngami ... bye bye ... bye bye.

Zandile now enters the acting area. She is quite subdued and she looks a bit sad and apprehensive as she faces the rest of her journey homeward on her own. She starts singing about mothers who will be coming home bringing their children sweets, rice and meat. At first she sings the song to herself, but it grows more confident as she winds her way around the acting area as if it were her path home. She notices some pretty stones

1

on her path and stops to pick them up. She continues, now playing a hop-scotch game with the stones. She slows down as she sings ...

ZANDILE: Nabaya omame, bethwel' imithwalo
            Nabaya omame, bethwel' imithwalo
            Ngcingci bo, ngcingci bo, nabaya omame
            Sabona ngoricey, sabona ngonyama
            Sabona ngokhekhe, sabona ngoswitie

            Mhhhm swities! I wonder if my
            grandmother will bring me some sweets
            today ... lucky if she does because she will
            bring me my favourite icemints! That's what
            I like. I could be standing here like this and
            my gogo would say to me – Zandi, I have a
            surprise for you. Close your eyes, open your
            mouth ...

She closes her eyes and opens her mouth for Gogo to put something in it. Her eyes grow bigger with the thought of the sweets and she pops a stone into her mouth. She imagines that it has become her favourite sweet.

ZANDILE: Mmmm ... icemints. *(She succeeds in her
            fantasy for one moment, but once again the
            sweet becomes a stone, and she spits it out).*
            Ag phu! Ngiyisilima kanti akunaswidi la it's
            just a stone!

Suddenly in her imagination she hears a little girl laughing at her. She turns around and focusses her attention where the imaginary child is seated.

2

ZANDILE: What are you laughing at wena? Uthini? I know it was just a stone. I am not stupid. And I am not talking to myself! Maybe you have got lots of friends to play with, but I don't ... You also don't have anybody to play with? You can play with me. You could be my friend. What's your name? *(Pause)* Bongi – that's a nice name.

Mina nginguZandile ... I'm so glad I found you Bongi, you are going to be my own friend and you will play with me everyday when I come back from school.

Where do you stay? *(Pauses and listens as if the child is answering her)* At our house? Ooh Bongi, but how come I've never seen you before? *(Pause)* Yes, we are wearing the same shoes *(laughs)*. I like your dress though. Jo! Those goats! They are beautiful Bongi. I wish I had a dress like that too. And who plaits your hair for you? *(Zandi is wide-eyed with shock and envy)* You plait your own hair ... everyday before you go to school! Hayi uclever wena.

Which school do you go to? *(Pauses and listens as if the child is answering her)* Why do you go to a school like that? That is a bad school. My father would never let me go there. You must change and come to my school now that you are my friend. *(Pause, as if Bongi is arguing for her school)* I know somebody there ... you know what they did? This girl, she was only sick, she stays next door to me, and they beat her up *(demonstrating)* and they beat her up until her hands were so swollen ... they thought

3

she was dodging school but she wasn't, she was sick. I'll never go there where they beat you so much. Ngeke!

(Zandi has been talking so much she doesn't see Bongi take out some sweets) Bongi? Who bought you those sweets? *(Pause)* I wish I had one. You won't give me? *(Pause as she goes to get one from Bongi)* Thank you Bongi, and the thing is nobody is going to see you, I'm the only one who's going to see you, only when I want to see you. It's just the two of us. *(They hold hands)*

(Zandile draws some circles on the floor to prepare for a game) Come, let's play amagendo. You don't know how to play it? But how old are you? *(Excitement)* Eight! I'm also eight. *(Pause)* I am eight Bongi. I know people think I'm ten because I'm so tall. *(Pause)* I am tall, I'm taller than you. Come, let's stand back to back. *(She backs up and starts measuring with the flat of her hand against her head and Bongi's)* Bongi, don't stand on tip toe, he-e uyarobha wena, I'm not playing with you anymore, I am not pla - yi - ngi! *(Bongi apologises and promises not to cheat anymore)*

Look at my feet, let's stand like this – you see, I am taller! One day, I'm going to be a tall teacher, like Miss Dlamini, and walk like this *(demonstrates)* hee ngiqhenye habe ... What will you become when you grow up? *(Pause)* Jo! A white lady! That is nice Bongi, we can still be friends. I'll be a tall teacher and you will be a white lady with long hair

4

like that, and you will have nice clothes and nice shoes with high heels ... and, and you can put rudge on your lips njengalomlungu wakaWebber ... but I don't like it so much ... And Bongi, we can speak English – Ismasdat lapetelez for you? And I can say – Was da meta be you? *(Stops and thinks)* Bongi, you can also have a car! Unginike ilift sihambe sobabili sigqoke kahle abantu basibuke bathi ... hish mame, qhaks baby. We can go anywhere together! Come Bongi, let's sing.

Nabaya omame, bethwel' imithwalo
Nabaya omame, bethwel' imithwalo
Ngcingi bo, ngcingci bo, nabaya omame
Sabona ngoswidi, sabona ngokhekhe
Sabona ngoricey, sabona ngonyama
Ngcingi bo, ngcingci bo, nabaya omame ...

Carried away by the excitement of the moment, Bongi and Zandi sing their way off the stage.

SCENE TWO

GRANDMOTHER (GOGO) AT HOME

Gogo returns from shopping in town with Zandile. She puts down the packets and goes out to the stoep to greet her neighbour. The neighbour is a little distance away, so Gogo calls to her

GOGO: Sawubona weMaGumede! *(Laughs)* Ninjani? Sisaphila. No I have just arrived ... You mean from the weekend? Oh! I came back last night. I really had a good time. Dundee is a beautiful little town. Hayi, *(looking at her dress)* me? Looking good? No, I'm getting too old now (laughs) but not too old to travel. I really had a good time. Bye bye. *(Half to herself)* It's always nice to come back home.

Humming a church song, Gogo looks through the window and sees Zandile playing with other children. She turns and starts unpacking the shopping bags. A new doll falls out. Gogo picks it up and chuckles to herself as she looks at the doll, remembering ...

GOGO: Oh, my grandchild. What did she say to me the other day when I bought this doll? Hawu Gogo, I love this doll but why do they always make them pink? *(She laughs)*

I hope Zandile is happy living with me. Oh, I could not bear to see the child playing all by herself looking so subdued. And there I was, with all the time in the world. Why could my grandchild be lonely? And yes, I have been lonely too since my husband died and my son Tom moved out with his family.

I would not talk badly about Tom, but he is the one who should take care of Zandile. His wife's hands are full – she has to take take of their six children. Zandile's own mother lives in the Transkei with her husband and four children. So Zandile is nobody's responsibility it seems. Well, she's welcome to be my responsibility. Oh, she's such a delight to cook for. *(Pauses, thinking)*

And is she clever! You should see her at the shops. She reads that shopping list so well. She is really a clever little girl. She could become a doctor, or a lawyer or an accountant. *(Excited)* She could be anything. And I'm here to help her with her homework, and tell her stories. Her father used to love my stories.

Am I glad I work! With Tom's two boys ready to go to college, I could smell trouble. I asked him to let Zandile come and stay with me because I thought if he ran short of money, Zandile would be the first to be taken out of school.

8

Tom thinks education is not important for a girl. Ha! Even if I have to die doing it, I'm keeping Zandile at school.

ZANDILE'S LIFE WITH GOGO

We see Zandile and her grandmother's lives together. They each thrive on this relationship. Grandmother gives the child the great gift of stories and the magic to tell them, and the child gives the grandmother a purpose.

Zandile and her grandmother enter stage left, down the passage. They have just returned from West Street, where Grandmother had taken Zandile shopping. It is Zandile's first time in the big city.

ZANDILE: Kungeve kumnandi edrobheni Gogo, and I had nice ice-cream.

GOGO: You had three ice-creams!

ZANDILE: Futhi ngadla nobhanana omude ongaka, I like banana, and Gogo, do you remember when we got a lift korisho? I thought I was going to fall at the back when he started to run with us. Gogo, wena awuzisabi izimpondo zakhe ezinkulu kangaka?

GOGO: Oh, I know you are so excited ... Come, sit down now. I must get you something to drink.

ZANDILE:	Sizophuzani weGogo?
GOGO:	Milk.
ZANDILE:	Can I have lemonade weGogo?
GOGO:	No no no no, you must have milk. Do you know what's going to happen if you don't drink milk? Your teeth will fall out. Your bones will be so weak, you won't be able to walk. I don't want my grandchild to be like that. Milk for you. *(She exits centre as if to go to the kitchen)*
ZANDILE:	WeGogo?
GOGO:	*(Off)* Yebo.
ZANDILE:	When are we going to the beach?
GOGO:	No, no, I am too old to swim now.
ZANDILE:	I know Gogo, but you can take me and you can sit at the beach and you can put your feet in the water and I will do all the swimming. *(Gogo returns with Zandile's milk in a cup and a glass of sherry on a tray)*
GOGO:	Okay, we'll go to the beach, but first drink up your milk now. And Granny's going to have a little sherry.
ZANDILE:	Gogo, are you drinking lemonade?
GOGO:	Yes.
ZANDILE:	Can I have some?
GOGO:	When you've finished your milk you can drink lemonade.
ZANDILE:	Gogo, amakhekhe?
GOGO:	I nearly forgot, I have some cakes. Would you like some? *(Gogo leaves stage. Zandile takes a quick gulp of 'lemonade', chokes and returns to her seat, drinking all her milk. Gogo re-enters with a tin of mazawatee tea filled with Eet-sum-more biscuits)* Good girl,

	you are drinking your milk. Do you want some lemonade?

ZANDILE: Gogo I don't want lemonade I like my milk. *(She imitates the pose on the biscuit tin of 'Happy Family')* Angithi Gogo yithi sobabili laba?

GOGO: Yes, just the two of us. *(Laughs)* These biscuits ... do you like them? *(Zandile nods)* Do you know what they are called? Eet-sum-more. Do you know what that means?

ZANDILE: Does it mean you can eat one and another and another and another and the tin never goes empty?

GOGO: Ake uveze izincwadi phela ngibone. Show me your books. What were you doing this week at school?

ZANDILE: Kade senza izibalo i-arithmetic mina ngathola ten out of ten. Ngisayolanda incwadi yami ngikubonise.

Buka ke, I got correct, correct, correct, and my teacher wrote good. And you know what else we did, we said poems and played some nice games we know.

GOGO: And what did you do?

ZANDILE: I played this game: 'Ngake ngahamba, ngahamba wema.' Wena-ke Gogo uzothi 'Two Sheleni'. Asenze-ke.

GOGO: O ... O

ZANDILE: Ngake ngahamba, ngahamba wema.

GOGO: Two Sheleni.

ZANDILE: Ngahlangana nezinsizw' ezimbili.

GOGO: Three Sheleni.

ZANDILE:	*(Gogo has made a mistake)* Eh-eh Gogo. Two Sheleni njalo, njalo.
GOGO:	O ... O. Njalo, njalo?
ZANDILE:	*(Starts again)* Ngake ngahamba, ngahamba wema.
GOGO:	Two sheleni.
ZANDILE:	Ngahlangana nezinsizw' ezimbili.
GOGO:	Two sheleni.
ZANDILE:	Zangimisa zangibingelela.
GOGO:	Two sheleni.
ZANDILE:	Zangibuz' igama lami wema.
GOGO:	Two sheleni.
ZANDILE:	Ngazitshela ngathi nginguZandile.
GOGO:	Two sheleni.
ZANDILE:	Zangibuza zathi ntomb' ungowaphi.
GOGO:	Two sheleni.
ZANDILE:	Ngazitshela ngathi ngingowakaMthembu, kaQhudeni kaMvelase, kaMpofane, owawel' uThukela ngobindlala iwile.
GOGO:	Two sheleni. *(She starts clapping enthusiastically)* O...!
ZANDILE:	Eh-eh Gogo, I'm not finished!
GOGO:	I'm sorry.
ZANDILE:	Zangibuza zathi ntomb' uqomephi.
GOGO:	Two sheleni.
ZANDILE:	Ngazitshela ngathi angikakaqomi, ngiseyingane, yesikole, yesikole, yesikole!
GOGO:	Hawu! And you say you learnt this song about boyfriends from your teacher?
ZANDILE:	No Gogo. Sis Kate did it at the wedding last month. I can't do it as good as she, but I'm going to be good. Angithi Gogo?

GOGO: Mntanomntanami, you are very, very good, and now I have a little surprise for you, for being so good at school.

ZANDILE: Oh, Gogo, I'm going to stay with you forever because you always have surprises. *(Gogo takes a small packet of sweets called 'Zulu Mottos' out of her handbag)*

GOGO: You make me so happy! Here, Zulu Mottos.

ZANDILE: Gogo, I like Zulu Mottos. *(She puts the sweet straight into her mouth)*

GOGO: Eh-eh, read it first!

ZANDILE: Yebo Gogo ... *(she reads)*

GOGO: What does it say?

ZANDILE: Elami libhalwe ukuthi ene, 'Ndlebenkulu'. Hawu Gogo, does that mean I'm going to have big ears after eating it?

GOGO: Bakithi, no no no, it's just a playful writing! Give me one too, please.

ZANDILE: Yebo, Gogo ... what does yours say?

GOGO: Uyisithandwa somphefumulo wami – you are the love of my heart.

ZANDILE: Asho mina angithi Gogo? WeGogo, is it true that there is somebody on the moon?

GOGO: Yes, there is someone on the moon.

ZANDILE: Are you going to tell me a story? *(Excited)*

GOGO: In fact, I do have a little story about that ... You see there was this woman. She always woke up early in the morning just after the cock crowed for the third time.

ZANDILE: *(Imitates a cock crowing)* Lithi kukulukugu.

GOGO: Yes, she would go to the river to fetch some water for her family.

ZANDILE: Why did she go to the river? Did they have no water taps in the house?

GOGO: Mntanomntanami, in those times nobody had any water taps. And they also had to make a fire to warm the water so they could wash. The woman got up early one winter morning, it was freezing cold, and saw that there was no firewood to make fire. It was a Sunday and she knew that she was not allowed to chop wood or do any work on a Sunday.

ZANDILE: Gogo, they also told us that at Sunday school.

GOGO: But she had a baby and she could not wash that small baby in cold water. Again the husband and the baby would need some food as well. So she thought she would quickly get some firewood before anyone could see her. She took the baby and tied it to her back, took some ropes and set off, walking very fast. Their dog followed them.

ZANDILE: Gogo, what was the dog's name?

GOGO: Baxakile ...

ZANDILE: And what colour was it, Gogo?

GOGO: Green ... with pink spots and a red nose and a purple tail and big green eyes.

ZANDILE: Gogo, I wish I was living in the olden days.

GOGO: Why?

ZANDILE: So that I could have a dog like that.

GOGO: Oh, Mntanomntanami, it's a pity because they don't make them like that anymore.

ZANDILE: If I had a dog like that, I could take it to town and to school with me and I could ...

GOGO: Can I go on with my story now?

ZANDILE:	Yebo, Gogo.
GOGO:	So she collected quite a bit of firewood and made a bundle. She carried it on her head and went back home. She was still on her way when she felt dizzy like she was walking in a dream. But she did not know what was happening. So people say she was punished and sent up to the moon with her baby on her back, the bundle of wood on her head and the dog behind her.
ZANDILE:	*(Very sleepy now)* I wonder what happened to the father and the grandmother and the other people.
GOGO:	It was a shame because they never saw her again and the father and the grandmother never had the pleasure of watching the baby grow into a beautiful, clever little girl like you! That is why when the moon is full you can see a woman on the moon ... so that people can see and learn. *(Gogo now looks down at Zandile, who has rested her head on her grandmother's lap. Zandile has fallen asleep)*
GOGO:	Sleepy ... sleepy. Come Mntanomntanami, you must go to bed now. *(She gently wakes up Zandile)*
ZANDILE:	Is the story finished now, Gogo?
GOGO:	Yes, I even started another one. Come, you can go to bed now.
ZANDILE:	Goodnight Gogo. *(Offstage)* Gogo.
GOGO:	Okay, your pyjamas are under your pillow.
ZANDILE:	Gogo are you coming to sleep with me? *(Pause)* Gogo, when are you coming to bed? *(Sounding very sleepy)*

GOGO:	As soon as I finish tidying up here.
ZANDILE:	Gogo, can I start praying now?
GOGO:	*(She starts the prayer while tidying up)* Yebo, UJehova unguMalusi wami ...
ZANDILE:	*(Even more sleepy)* UJehova unguMalusi wami ...
GOGO:	Angiyikweswela ...
ZANDILE:	Angiyikweswela ...
GOGO:	Ungilalisa emadlelweni aluhlaza ...
ZANDILE:	Ungilalisa emadlelweni aluhla ... *(her voice fades away. She has fallen asleep)*

SCENE FOUR (a)

ZANDILE TEACHES FLOWERS

Zandile enters in her new dress. She addresses the grandmother's flowerbeds as if the flowers are a class of children and she is the teacher. She has a small stick in her hand.

ZANDILE: Ho ho ho ho! Good morning class! Good morning, Miss Zandile. And what was all that noise I was hearing down the passage? Poor Miss Bongi could hardly teach her Standard Twos. She teaches Nature Study, you know, she's very clever. But do you know what happens to naughty children? The white car will come for you and you won't even know it's coming. It's going to be standing there and it will be too late to run. Nobody can hear you scream because its engine makes such a loud noise. They're going to take out your eyes and take you to a far away place and nobody's going to see you ever again. *(She pauses as if she is listening to something)* And what is that I'm hearing ... is that the white car? Ho ho ho ho! No, you are lucky this time. But I'm going to send you straight to the principal's office and he is going to give you this *(she demonstrates a hiding with her stick)*.

Wena, and you are chewing gum in class. *(She holds out her hand)* Give it to me. I am going to put it on your naughty, naughty little face. Teach you! And the rest of you must listen to me! And how do you like my new dress? This is a new dress, and my grandmother bought it for me and she let me choose it all by myself. I chose it because of all the goats and the giraffes and the elephants. It is very important for you to be clean, and look at you, you've got grass on your hair. Don't you know what day it is today? It is the 21st of September 1966 and the inspector is coming here today. You know the inspector does not understand our language *(she starts giggling)* and we don't want to embarrass him. *(Puts her hand over her mouth and laughs)* He cannot say our real names so we must all use white names in class today. Hands up those of you who don't have white names. We'll just have to give them to you. Wena you can be Violet. *(She points to different setions of the audience each time she mentions a different flower)* Petunia. Daisy. Sunflower and Innocentia ... I don't know what that means ... Do you know what name the inspector gave me in class today? Elsie. And I don't even look like an Elsie! Don't laugh! At least you are flowers. And do you know what he called Bongi? Moses! He couldn't even tell that she is a girl.

Now where was I? Good morning class. Good morning Miss Zandile. What can we do today? We could sing! This could be a singing class ... if we get it right we can sing for the inspector, but if we get it wrong, then the white car will come for us. Now where are you noise makers, you Violets, because you are always shrieking – you can sing soprano – mmhh! *(Humming a note for them to sing)* And you my lovely Daisies, are my favourites! You never make any noise – just like me, you will sing alto, because I'm alto too. *(Hums a note)* And my little Petunias, those compositions you wrote were top class, you can sing tenor ... mhhhmm! *(Hums a note. Each time she hums the notes get lower)* Good! And you Sunflowers, you are such a disappointment, so tall and you are still in Sub A. Honestly, this is because your voices are broken already – Booaah! *(She struggles getting a deep bass note, and starts walking like Miss Dlamini. She has a problem climbing the big box where she stands to conduct her choir, but as soon as she succeeds, she pulls herself together)*

The song is called Hamba kahle Vuyelwa *(She enunciates the title again)* Hamba – kahle – Vuyelwa

1, 2, 3, 4

Hamba Kahle Vuyelwa
Usikhonzele emzini
Kwandonga ziyaduma
Inkos' isikelele
Inkos' ithamsanqele

Hamba Vuyelwa!

Very good, let's do it again. *(She's very pleased. She starts singing, but the song breaks down)* You don't want to sing nina, he? You think I'm a fool opening my mouth like this ha ha ha nx! Let's do it again ... *(Tearfully)* Hamba kahle Vuyelwa ... *(This time the sunflowers make a mistake and she cannot take it anymore, she climbs down to give them all a hiding, breaking the flowers in the process)*

You children don't want to sing. I'll teach you. *(Beats the ground with her stick)* He-e man, I'm not your friend, you are not my friends anymore, I'm going to call the white car for you ...

SCENE FOUR (b)

ZANDILE WITH GOGO IN THE GARDEN

The grandmother enters, having heard all the noise.

GOGO: Hawu ... hawu Zandile! What are you doing breaking my flowers?

ZANDILE: But Gogo, these children don't want to sing the way I tell them to.

GOGO: Zandile, you can teach them if you like, but don't beat them. How will they grow? Hawu Zandile!

ZANDILE: I'm sorry, Gogo, ngiyacela ungangishayi ...

GOGO: Okay, okay, nobody is going to hit you. You must sing as well, so that they can learn from you. How would you like it, if I hit you with a stick, as hard as you were hitting them?

ZANDILE: I'm sorry. I didn't know that they could feel, Gogo ...

GOGO: You must remember one thing, everything that grows has feelings. Now sing to them, the way you would like them to sing.

ZANDILE: Eh-eh. Angifuni. I've been teaching them the whole day.

GOGO:	Then Gogo's going to teach them a new song. *(She starts singing)* Vuka vuka Zola sesifikile – Ah ... *(She notices that Zandile has moved closer to her, and seems to want to sing the song)* Oh, so you also want to sing now?
ZANDILE:	Yebo Gogo!
GOGO:	Alright, let me teach you. *(She sings very slowly, emphasizing the words and melody, so that Zandile can learn the song)* Vuka – Vuka – Zola – Sesifikile – Ah – Ulele na – Ulele na *(Zandile joins in on the odd words when she feels confident with a note or word)* Sogibel' ibhasi – Zola – Siy' eThekwini – Ah – Ulele na – Ulele na – Sobon' ulwandle – Zola – Lugubh' amagagasi – Ah – Ulele na – Ulele na.
GOGO:	Very good. Now let's try.
ZANDILE:	Yebo Gogo.
TOGETHER:	Vuka Vuka Zola
	Sesifikile ah
	Ulele na ulele na
	Sogibel' ibhasi Zola
	Siy' eThekwini ah
	Ulele na ulele na
	Sobon' ulwandle Zola
	Lugubh' amagagasi ah
	Ulele na ulele ... *(Gogo gestures to Zandile that she should sing a higher harmony)*
	Ah ulele na
	Ulele ah
	Ulele na
	Ulele ah ...

GOGO:	*(As they finish)* You see, we can all sing together.
ZANDILE:	WeGogo, I want to sing again.
GOGO:	No, no. I think that's enough for today. It's a special day tomorrow. Go and polish your shoes now.
ZANDILE:	And shine them until I see my face on them!
GOGO:	Do you know that tomorrow is a special day?
ZANDILE:	What Gogo? I'm going to the beach – ngci ngci!
GOGO:	It's the end of the term and ...
ZANDILE:	It's a surprise!
GOGO:	Yes Gogo Mthwalo is going on holiday to Port Shepstone.
ZANDILE:	Is your overcoat coming with you? Ibhantshi lakho liyakulandela, angithi Gogo?
GOGO:	Of course my little overcoat is coming with me.
ZANDILE:	I want to start packing now!
GOGO:	Why do you think they call me 'Gogo Mthwalo Uboshiwe'?
ZANDILE:	Because your bags are already ready. Are we going now?
GOGO:	No, you still have one more day at school.
ZANDILE:	My new dress is not packed, can I wear it to school tomorrow?
GOGO:	Are you going to pass tomorrow?
ZANDILE:	Yebo, I did work hard!
GOGO:	Alright, you can wear your dress!
ZANDILE:	And can I wear my neckless to school?
GOGO:	Neckless? Okay!
ZANDILE:	And my earrings and my bangles, Gogo?
GOGO:	Okay!

ZANDILE:	And my hairpins, Gogo?
GOGO:	Okay! And can you do something for Gogo?
ZANDILE:	Yebo Gogo.
GOGO:	Go and polish your shoes!

Zandile exits, laughing, while the grandmother remains on stage to tidy up.

GOGO: Oh! My grandchild ... I can even see my little Zandile, wearing a white dress, walking slowly out of church with her husband and smiling with those dimples that I like. And I can see the neighbours watching with envy. Then I'll come out, sweeping the whole yard with a new broom – lililili! Kwakuhle kwethu, uthini wemfazi ongazalanga, halala!

She sweeps her way out of the stage.

SCENE FIVE

THE WHITE CAR COMES FOR ZANDILE

Gogo's ululation can still be heard in the background. Zandile enters, singing happily on her way back from school. It's the last day and she has passed her exams. She knows that Gogo will give her a present.

ZANDILE: Khilikithi
Khilikithi khilikithi
Zandile uphasile
Uzothol' ipresenti
Khilikithi khilikithi
Zandile uphasile
Uzohamba noGogo
Baye ePort Shepstone
Khilikithi khilikithi

She sings until she gets home, where she leaves her books and goes out to play. She notices a white car idling towards her. She stops singing abruptly. As if somebody has come out of the car and is advancing towards her, she retreats accordingly.

ZANDILE: Bongi, stay next to me. It's the white car. I'm scared. Sawubona ... No, I've got my own sweets from Gogo ... No! I don't want to go with you. Gogo's taking me on holiday to Port Shepstone. Gogo wouldn't want me to go with people I don't know. *(Pause)* No, you're not! *(She is trapped against the back wall)* Bongi, go and tell my grandmother the white car has come for me, go tell my brother Paul, please Bongi, run! *(She screams)*

Then as if she is being pulled into the car, she lunges forward, screaming as she reaches the end of the stage.

SCENE SIX

GOGO DISCOVERS ZANDILE IS GONE

The grandmother enters. She is humming happily to herself and is carrying a beautifully wrapped present. She has been shopping.

GOGO: Zandi, I'm home ... Zandile, I'm home my little one and I have a present for you. Ntombizandile! Usebuyile uMthwalo Uboshiwe. UMthwalo Uzethule. Siyahamba namhlanje we are going to Port Shepstone today – where is my little overcoat? If you don't come I'm cancelling the trip. I'm so tired, come and give Granny a big hug ... Zandile! I'm not playing hide and seek today I'm too tired, just come out. Zandi! Zandile! *(She notices the school satchel on the ground)*

Zandi! Just because we are going on holiday she is throwing things around. *(She picks up the satchel, sits down, opens the satchel and finds Zandile's report card and reads it)* Oooo! She passed. Three gold stars! Bakithi! *(She reads)* Zandile is quiet

29

and well mannered in class. With a little more effort she is capable of producing work of a very high standard. Ooo! My grandchild! ... Zandile, how can I give you your present if you don't come out? Little feet under the bed, game is over now. *(She is getting really worried)* This is strange ... wait, let me ask MaGumede *(she calls her neighbour)*

MaGumede! ... Have you seen Zandile? ... Yes ... Who? ... Where? A white car? No, I didn't ask anyone to take her! Oh my God. *(Crying)* What am I going to do now? I never instructed anyone to take her ... What am I going to say to her father? Oh Zandile!

Towards the end of this speech a police siren and a radio announcement are heard

Announcer: Attention! We interrupt this programme with an important news flash. A little girl has gone missing from her grandmother's home in Hammersdale. She was last seen at about 2.30 this afternoon, getting into a white car, type and registration not known. The child is eight years old, she speaks Zulu, her name is Zandile and she was wearing a yellow dress, with animal and flower patterns on it. Anyone who may have any information at all as to her whereabouts, is requested to contact the nearest police station or the child's grandmother Mrs Zwide, at the Hammersdale Police Station.

The voices of Zandile and Gogo fade in, singing Vuka Vuka on
a pre-recorded tape

> Vuka Vuka Zola
> Sesifikile ah
> Ulele na
> Sogibel' ibhasi Zola
> Siy' eThekwini ah
> Ulele na
> Sobon' ulwandle Zola
> Lugubha amagagasi ah
> Ulele na
> Ulele na ulele na ulele na.

During the radio announcement Gogo leaves the stage to fetch
a large, well travelled suitcase. She re-enters, and into it, she
lovingly packs the brightly gift-wrapped presents that she had
bought for Zandile, but can now no longer give her. By now the
tape recording of the song Vuka Vuka is playing. She slowly and
sadly leaves the stage.

SCENE SEVEN

GOGO SEARCHES FOR ZANDILE AND ZANDILE'S LETTER TO GOGO

Zandile is writing letters to her grandmother on the sand with a large stick. Her hope is that the birds, that fly so far, will take the words she has written to her grandmother. In this way her need to communicate with her grandmother is expressed, and to a degree satisfied, particularly when she goes to check the next day and finds that the words have gone.

ZANDILE: Dear Gogo. How are you? I'm still not happy in this place. You must come and fetch me now. Always when I write to you, they tear the letters, now I hope if I write like this, on the sand, the birds will see this letter and bring it to you. They are my friends and talk to me all the time. Maybe if you can talk with them, they will bring me a message from you. I don't get time to play anymore, there are so many chores to do.

        Maybe it's good for me, maybe it can make me strong.

And you know what? Yesterday I had to chop wood before I went to school, and I got a splinter in my hand, and blisters. When I told my mother, she said I was making excuses for being lazy. During lunch break at school my teacher saw me crying and she took the splinter out for me. She put Zambuk on my blisters, and that reminded me of you. They don't have Zambuk here. *(Zandile becomes quite enthusiastic now)*

My teacher, I like her. Her name is Miss Maduma. She is very clever. I always come first in all my subjects. I am very lucky because she takes all my classes. I will show you my report and test books. *(Zandile lies down as if to rest)*

The grandmother re-enters, with a photograph of Zandile in her hand. She asks members of the audience:

GOGO: Have you seen this child? *(Showing the photograph)* Have you seen her? Her name is Zandile. *(She moves to others)* She is eight years old, she disappeared on the 14th December 1966. She was wearing a little dress with animals on it. *(She moves on)* Have you seen Zandile?

Just as she begins to leave the auditorium ...

ZANDILE: But soon now, I must go and cut grass for thatch for the roof. And it's very far to walk to fetch the grass. And Gogo, when you come please can you bring me some shoes.

They won't let me wear them here. They only wear shoes when they go to church. Do you think that God can see their shoes under the benches? I must still wear the ones you bought me and they are too small now and old and the children always laugh at the way these shoes make me walk.

They also laughed at me when I didn't know how to put cow dung on the floor. They said I was making funny faces when I did not like the smell. But I can do it much better now and I always help them when it's their turn. And Gogo when we are in the fields with other children, and the parents are far away, I always tell them stories. I told them all the stories you told me. And they say I am very lucky to have someone like you. Gogo I can make up my own stories now, but I miss you very very very much Gogo, but I know that you love me and you'll come and fetch me.

Obebhala
Zandile

SCENE EIGHT

ZANDILE WITH MOTHER IN THE FIELD

Lulama enters centre stage

LULAMA: Uphi Zandile? Where are you? What are you doing? It's getting late and you must still cut more grass.

ZANDILE: Hawu Mama, I'm afraid of the mice.

LULAMA: What are they going to do? Are they going to eat you up? *(Sees the letter)* And what is this ... this child is full of dreams. *(She rubs the letter out with her feet. Zandile and Lulama mime cutting grass with sickles. Lulama looks up at Zandile)* Zandile bend lower. You must cut the grass at the bottom.

ZANDILE: The grass is cutting my hands Mama.

LULAMA: I don't know what to do with this child now.

ZANDILE: And you don't know what to do with me.

LULAMA: I want you to grow up and be a strong woman and ...

ZANDILE: I'm going to be a teacher.

LULAMA: Not here. You have to work outside here, where the men can see you.

ZANDILE:	Men can still see me if I teach.
LULAMA:	Where are you going to teach here? Are you going to teach the goats? Sit down. I want to talk to you. What are you doing?
ZANDILE:	*(Mumbles, scratching her left leg)* The grass is itchy Mama.
LULAMA:	Sukugeza! *(Zandile gets up as if to leave the stage)* Where are you going?
ZANDILE:	You told me to go and wash.
LULAMA:	Tyhini bethuna! I didn't say go and wash. I only said don't be silly. You are not good for me if you are doing this. In a few years you have to be married. Who do you think you are going to marry if you can't do a woman's work?
ZANDILE:	I'm not going to get married. I am very good at school.
LULAMA:	What are you going to do with this education? All you have to be is a good wife and have good children. That's what I want from you.
ZANDILE:	I don't want to.
LULAMA:	This is not Durban, this is the Transkei. Here you must stop arguing with me. You must shut up when I speak. Zandile, listen to me. I was talking to Matshezi the other day. Do you know her son?
ZANDILE:	Yebo Mama.
LULAMA:	His family wants you.
ZANDILE:	But I don't want him.
LULAMA:	What do you mean you don't want him? His uncle has the richest family in this village. He could have any girl in the village and he

	chose you. That's how I got married as well. You must have your own house.
ZANDILE:	But I don't like him. He's got all these ugly scars on his face.
LULAMA:	But that's our tradition! *(She notices Zandile scratching her back)*
LULAMA:	What's wrong with you now?
ZANDILE:	My back is so sore from the bending.
LULAMA:	Why are you so lazy? First your hands get cut by grass and then your legs are itchy – now it's your back! How do you think you will build your own house if you don't let your hands get used to it? Look at mine. I've been cutting grass every winter – ever since I was your age. I cut the grass for every roof in this house.
ZANDILE:	I don't like thatch roofs anyway. I like the roof my grandmother had in Durban.
LULAMA:	Life is different here. No time for rest – just work. If you learn that then you will make a good wife for Matshezi's son.
ZANDILE:	I don't know why you took me from Gogo, if you are just going to give me away to Matshezi's son.
LULAMA:	Zandile I took you because you are my child.
ZANDILE:	But you don't even let me visit my grandmother.
LULAMA:	I can't because if I let you go there, you will never come back again. I know you were happy there, I saw you that night.
ZANDILE:	You saw me Mama?
LULAMA:	Yes, when I went to visit your grandmother in Durban. *(Sits)* I wanted to take you then, but I knew Gogo would never let you go,

	after all those years you had become her child.
ZANDILE:	But you shouldn't have stolen me.
LULAMA:	How else was I going to get you? Wait till you have a child, you'll know what I've been going through all the years. How do you think it feels, to know that your child doesn't even know you exist?
ZANDILE:	But Ma, I'm only 12, why are you in such a hurry to give me away, if you missed me so much?
LULAMA:	But it's our tradition. It was the same when I got married. By the time I was 22, I already had four children.
ZANDILE:	But I don't even like him.
LULAMA:	You don't have to like him, he has to like you. Do you think I was happy with my husband? But he chose me. I had to stay married to him.
ZANDILE:	But he left you.
LULAMA:	It's easy for men to go.
ZANDILE:	And you also left me all those years.
LULAMA:	I left you because I had to. Do you think my husband would have accepted you? He would have killed me if had come to his home with another man's child. My going to find work in Durban was bad enough – even though he knew I was forced to because he was not bringing us any money. He would beat me if I asked for money. My mother said I must go and find work while she was still able to look after my children. So I went to Durban and because my papers were not in order, it was hard to find work. And when I did get work they could pay me anything

	they liked. I got two pounds a month. Even in those days it was nothing.
ZANDILE:	Was that before I was born?
LULAMA:	Yes, 1958 ... *(pause)* That was a difficult year for me. Then something happened, I bumped into an old friend that I grew up with here. Dudu looked so happy and beautiful and I could see that she had a good job.
ZANDILE:	She was a teacher?
LULAMA:	No, she was a singer with a successful group called 'Mtateni Queens', and one of their singers had just left the band, so Dudu asked me if I would like to join so I joined the group.
ZANDILE:	*(Holding back laughter)* Haai bo wena!
LULAMA:	Yes, before Dudu left here we used to sing together for all the weddings, we were quite famous around here. There would never be a wedding without us singing. *(Does a bit of a wedding song)*
ZANDILE:	I wish I could have seen that.
LULAMA:	I thought I could earn better money, but it was hard work.
ZANDILE:	Harder work than here?
LULAMA:	*(Laughs)* Oho! Much harder and I had to send my money back to the Transkei for the children.
ZANDILE:	Why did you stay then?
LULAMA:	I stayed, hoping for better things to come, but they didn't. That is why I have learnt not to live on hopes, that is why I am teaching you to work. The sun is going down, it's time

41

to cook supper. Run and start the fire. I'll
call you back when the bundles are ready.

As Lulama mimes gathering the bundles, she starts to sing Mgewundini, a song she used to sing when she was on the cabaret circuit. As she picks up the last bundle, she stands and arches her back, and tries to rub away the pain.

SCENE NINE

ZANDI AND LINDI SWIM IN THE RIVER

Zandi runs on to the stage, jumps on to part of the set, as if it were a river bank. She looks down, as if into the water. She's very excited.

ZANDILE: Qops! I got here first. *(She turns as if she expects to see Lindiwe behind her. There is no Lindiwe)* Khawuleza man Lindi! Utsho ngokuba mde ngathi ngumntu endimthandayo. *(Laughs)* I got here first, you said you could run faster than I, but where are you now? I can run faster than you Lindiwe. I can't wait man. I wonder if Thekwane is here, last week when I was here I found this bird, Thekwane, looking at himself in the water. Ndimhle ngapha ndimbi ngapha, ndoniwa yilendawo. *(As she imitates the bird and turns around, Lindiwe jumps on to the stage, as if into the water, behind Zandile and gives her a big fright)*

LINDIWE: I got here first! Pe! *(Both in the water, they laugh and feel the water, splashing, holding their breath and noses. Still holding her nose,*

43

Zandile jumps as if into the water. They sit on the stage floor, with boxes around them so that all you can see of them are their heads and shoulders, to create the illusion that they are submerged in the river. Then Zandi starts to scream)

ZANDILE: Iyo, Iyo! Inyoka! It's the snake, it's bitten me.

LINDIWE: What?

ZANDILE: I thought I felt a snake at my feet.

LINDIWE: No, it's my feet kicking the water.

ZANDILE: I'm sure it was a snake.

LINDIWE: Hayi suka eligwala, inyoka yakwabani? There's no snake here.

ZANDILE: You know that snake scares me, nyani nyani. The other day, we were swimming here, you remember Nomthandazo, she was swimming with us, now she doesn't swim with us anymore.

LINDIWE: Why?

ZANDILE: Because the snake bit her, here in the water.

LINDIWE: He-ena wena, are you sure?

ZANDILE: I don't know, but ...

LINDIWE: But I've never seen a snake here! I suspect it's something else.

ZANDILE: Lindiwe it is the snake because she was swimming here with us, when she got out of the water we saw blood running down her legs. She told us Izilenzi bit her.

LINDIWE: Uyazi yintoni Zandi? *(Whispering confidently)* I suspect she could be sleeping with boys!

ZANDILE: *(Shocked)* Lindiwe! How do you know?

LINDIWE: I know because the other day in class she had blood coming out of her and she had to

44

	put a book under the skirt. She was so embarrassed. You should have seen her!
ZANDILE:	What did the teacher say?
LINDIWE:	He told her to go out of class. The teacher also knows that she is sleeping with boys. What would you do if you see blood?
ZANDILE:	I'd just wipe it.
LINDIWE:	O Yehova, andifuni nokuyicinga loo nto! I'd kill myself, what would they say at home?
ZANDILE:	Why do they think if you sleep with boys then you have blood?
LINDIWE:	I don't know, but I think it's true.
ZANDILE:	I wonder if the boys can also get it?
LINDIWE:	I want to ask my mother but I'm scared.
ZANDILE:	You can't! It's rude, tyhini unantoni kakade!
LINDIWE:	Why rude? Then how are we going to know for sure if we don't ask?
ZANDILE:	I just wish they would tell us those things.
LINDIWE:	I wonder where it comes from – you know umama kaGugu? Gugu told me that her mother is going to hospital.
ZANDILE:	Is she sick?
LINDIWE:	No, to get a baby.
ZANDILE:	They make babies esibhedlele?
LINDIWE:	Yes.
ZANDILE:	You know, my mother told me that babies come from the aeroplane.
LINDIWE:	Ha ha! When we want our babies we can get them from the hospital.
ZANDILE:	We can play with real babies.
LINDIWE:	And when we get tired ...
TOGETHER:	We take them back. *(They laugh and dip under the water)*

45

LINDIWE:	Let's go now, it's getting cold. Let's sit in the sun.
ZANDILE:	I hope my mother doesn't bring that Mama Matshezi to our house for tea.
LINDIWE:	Ha ha! Makoti kaMatshezi.
ZANDILE:	Just because his family has a lot of cattle! The boy is so ugly, if they ever send me to be his wife, I will have to run away.
LINDIWE:	I wish I could get married to somebody nice, but I hate the very long dresses married women wear, vhu-vhu-vhu – when they walk.
ZANDILE:	The other day when we took bundles of firewood to Matshezi's house, my mother was so happy and she made me dress up nicely so that that stupid boy could see me. I was so shy all the time and I had to work hard doing this, preparing that, so that the family could see how hard I can work.
LINDIWE:	Does the boy ever talk to you? Maybe he is a nice person even if he's ugly. You know what they say about a man – 'ubuhle bendoda'.
ZANDILE:	I find that very stupid. A man doesn't have to be good-looking but a girl has to be pretty. The ugliest man wants the most beautiful girl. Why?
LINDIWE:	I like to look pretty. I'm glad I'm a girl.
ZANDILE:	But when you are getting married you have to work even harder to look very special on that day, like Sis' Lulu at the wedding.
LINDIWE:	Oh *(she closes her eyes with her hands)* Zandile I've never seen anybody looking so beautiful, and she's got this round face and

	her teeth are snow white and a little mouth like a bird.
ZANDILE:	I know, I could never look like that even if I were to get married. I wonder what they did to her face.
LINDIWE:	They mix all kinds of herbs and I think the yellow of an egg and smear it all over the bride's face. Raw egg, lots of things and she has to stay inside. She hardly sees the sun. They prepare special food for her so that when she comes out ...
ZANDILE:	Aqhakaze axele ikhwezi lomso. I think the morning star that shines brightest at dawn is the most beautiful thing I've ever seen.
LINDIWE:	I know, but I hate waking up early in the morning, especially when it's winter.
ZANDILE:	Winter – hayi hayi my feet get so cold and they crack on the sides.
LINDIWE:	Zandile! Iminkenke? You must make ntyolantyola.
ZANDILE:	I don't know how to make it.
LINDIWE:	I know. You keep all the old pieces of candle, take out the twine inside and chop them to small pieces, put them in a tin on red-hot coals. When it's melted take it off and add some paraffin, stir it till it's cold, then you can just put it on your feet everyday when you finish washing them.
ZANDILE:	But it smells!
LINDIWE:	Not for long, it dries quickly.
ZANDILE:	I will try, I hate cracked feet.
LINDIWE:	Let's go now, it's getting cold!
ZANDILE:	Let's get back into the water! *(Zandile jumps back into the water. The resultant spray catches Lindiwe unawares. She screams and*

47

	then also jumps into the water) How come you've got bigger ... Your bells are bigger than mine. Sewunamabele amakhulu.
LINDIWE:	What? You know, I think I'm getting fat!
ZANDILE:	But you are getting big bells like your sister.
LINDIWE:	I don't know, and it's sore here.
ZANDILE:	Is it sore?
LINDIWE:	Yes *(rubbing them gently)*.
ZANDILE:	I wonder what happened? But why there?
LINDIWE:	I don't know, and I must stop eating chocolate because they say chocolate makes you fat.
ZANDILE:	But I eat all these things and my bells are not getting any bigger.
LINDIWE:	You'll always be skinny. Anyway I am bigger than you, that's why.
ZANDILE:	Have you slept with the boys?
LINDIWE:	No!
ZANDILE:	Is that why your bells are bigger than mine?
LINDIWE:	No! Who says if you sleep with boys you get fat? My mother checks me all the time and she knows I'm alright. *(Lindiwe sulks, Zandile touches her on the arm)*
ZANDILE:	Lindiwe ... *(Lindiwe pushes her away)* I am your friend. I know you have not slept with boys.
LINDIWE:	I'm just fat.
ZANDILE:	Yes, you're just fat. *(Uncomfortable silence, until Zandile changes the subject)* Lindiwe, you know what we can do? We can read books, we can read Bona and Drum and discover everything.
LINDIWE:	What do they say?

48

ZANDILE:	Lindiwe, I don't know. I haven't read them, but I've seen them.
LINDIWE:	I can steal some from my sister. And I can take them to school tomorrow.
ZANDILE:	The history class.
LINDIWE:	But ... but ... we can't ... the teacher will see them. I saw ... the other day, another girl was reading eeh ... True Love in class and the teacher beat and beat her.
ZANDILE:	But she should have put it inside the history book, man.
LINDIWE:	Oh, and she won't see it?
ZANDILE:	Ya.
LINDIWE:	Why the history book?
ZANDILE:	Because I hate history! The great trek, great trek, every year it is the same, the great trek. Nothing else ever happened here or anywhere, just the great trek. Yes, and so we put it in the history book, and we read, looking very serious.
LINDIWE:	Yes, I'll bring some tomorrow *(laughs)*.
ZANDILE:	We are going to read, discover everything. We are going to be grown ups *(she sneaks away)*.
LINDIWE:	*(Dives under the water, leaps up and screams, terrified)* Yo! Snake! *(She looks around, and under her breath ...)* Blood! Yo! Snake!

Blackout

SCENE TEN

ZANDILE GETS TO KNOW HER MOTHER

Zandile enters centre stage with goatskin, candle, notebook and pencil. She is singing Vuka Vuka softly to herself

LULAMA: *(Offstage)* Did you lock up the kitchen? Don't leave the candle burning.

ZANDILE: Ewe Ma. *(Lays out her goatskin, then looks over her shoulder to make sure that her mother isn't around. She hides the notebook and pencil under the goatskin. She lies down and sleeps. In her sleep ...)* Gogo, Gogo, Gogo. *(Lulama enters)*

LULAMA: Zandile, wake up! You are dreaming.

ZANDILE: Gogo?

LULAMA: This is your mother here.

ZANDILE: I thought I heard Gogo calling me.

LULAMA: There is no Gogo here, Zandile! Try to go back to sleep. *(Zandile gets up and moves away)*

LULAMA: Where are you going?

ZANDILE: I just want to sit here for a while.

LULAMA:	Zandile, is there something troubling you?
ZANDILE:	No, Ma.
LULAMA:	Well, just come here and sit with me. *(Pats bed, discovers it is wet)* Oh, Zandile, not again.
ZANDILE:	I don't know what else to do. Already I have stopped drinking anything from after lunch.
LULAMA:	What do you dream? Do you dream you want to go to the toilet and then you dream you are on the toilet? You must wake up just before ...
ZANDILE:	But Ma, I don't have these dreams.
LULAMA:	Are you sure you're not just being lazy to wake up?
ZANDILE:	No Ma, I also hate this thing – it embarrasses me.
LULAMA:	You must really try. In two years' time, everybody is expecting you to get married. And how am I going to give you to any man if you are wetting your bed? Oh Zandile *(lifting mat)* you'll have to remake your bed. What's this *(seeing the notebook and pencil, she picks up the notebook and flips the pages)* ... another letter, you still write when you know that your Gogo will never get them?
ZANDILE:	But they are my letters, and I know one day Gogo will come and fetch me.
LULAMA:	Fetch you where? She doesn't ... does she know where you are? Maybe if you forget your Gogo, you will stop wetting your bed!
ZANDILE:	I never used to wet my bed with Gogo, Gogo would have ...

LULAMA: Gogo, Gogo, Gogo! Zandile. I'm not going to argue with you. I'm tired *(as if she's leaving)*. I'm tired.

ZANDILE: People say if we slaughter a goat the ancestors will help me.

LULAMA: *(She stops and turns)* I know ... I have been thinking about that but you know that's impossible. Your father must be the one to do the ceremony. Even if I did it, it wouldn't help.

ZANDILE: Then Mama, maybe we must go to Durban.

LULAMA: With what money?

ZANDILE: We can write to my father to send us money.

LULAMA: And if he sends it do you think I would let you go alone? I can't go with you.

ZANDILE: This means I'll never go to Durban. Oh, why didn't you stay with my father because now I would have my mother and my father and my Gogo would be here with us, not like this here now.

LULAMA: Who says things will ever be like you want them to be? Who knows, one day you might see your father again.

ZANDILE: But Ma, I miss my father. You never talk about him.

LULAMA: Yes, I do think about him.

ZANDILE: He was a good man, andithi Ma?

LULAMA: Yes, I knew that from the first time I met him.

ZANDILE: Kuphi Ma?

LULAMA: In Durban.

ZANDILE: He was in your band?

LULAMA: No. I remember when I first met him. It was a Friday night and we were singing in one of the biggest shebeens eMkhumbane. It was packed full with people and our audience was really pleased. Then suddenly there was dead silence. Everybody looked towards the door – five men had just come in. They were all wearing oversized black suits and their shoes were shining. They had hats on, and people moved away nervously. I just wondered who they were but I kept on singing. People seemed to know there was going to be trouble – first a few people left then a few more followed and then the gang ordered us to sing 'Mgewundini' over and over. *(She sings a bit of it)* Do you know that song?

ZANDILE: Haai Mama.

LULAMA: You wouldn't know it. It was one of the popular songs those days.

ZANDILE: But Mama, was my father one of these men?

LULAMA: No! There was this tall well-dressed man who had been watching us since we started singing and he had been smiling at me all the time. I was looking at him when one of the gang came up on stage and grabbed me. I tried to fight him off but before I knew it, he was on the floor. That tall well-dressed man had knocked him down ... that was your father.

ZANDILE: He was brave, Mama!

LULAMA: And that's not all. He talked to the gang to let us go and they did. I couldn't believe it, a miracle. Tom became the friend of the group. I loved him. He was so different from my husband and kind. *(She is immediately embarrassed by her statement, and in the background, a cock crows)* Hamba

Zandile, I've been talking for the whole night. The sun is already coming up ... *(Zandile exits, taking her goatskin with her)*

I nearly made it. We were going to Johannesburg to cut a record and the people there were organising a tour for us. We were going to sing in Cape Town, P.E., East London and all the other lovely places. But then we had to tell them that I was four-months pregnant. Intoni, they wouldn't hear of it. They wanted me replaced. My friends stood for me but the organisers said they wouldn't have a pregnant woman on stage – as if it was such a disgrace, or as if I had made myself pregnant.

You know, at times I so wish that men could get pregnant too. All my hopes of improving my life and the lives of my children were finished. Tom and I agreed that I should stay in Durban until our child was born. I had a baby girl and we called her Zandile, Ntombi Zandile, which means the number of girls has grown.

She blows out the candle

SCENE ELEVEN

LINDIWE GOES TO JOHANNESBURG

Zandile enters. Letta Mbuli's "I'll Never Be The Same' is playing on the house radio. Zandile dances and sings with the music while she moves the 'furniture'. She then picks up Bona magazine and proceeds to read out loud one of the letters from the problems page. Letta Mbuli fades out.

ZANDILE: *(Reading)* Do you have a personal problem? Don't let it embarrass or worry you. Whether it be about love, sex, bad dreams, divorced parents or an unexpected pregnancy. Help is in sight. Dear Dolly I am in love with a girl who loves me dearly, but I keep hearing that her father was a thief until he went to the Holy Land. He has since changed but I don't know if she will follow in his footsteps. Confused. Port Elizabeth.

    (To herself) I wonder what Dolly will say to this.

Dear Confused. You can test your girl to see if she steals through various methods. If she does steal, things must be missing from your place, in most cases you can't

57

	judge a child by her father's behaviour, so don't let his reputation affect your decision about the daughter.
LINDIWE:	Zandile, uphi uZandile? Where are you?
ZANDILE:	Ngapha.
LINDIWE:	Zandile, usekhitshini, are you in the kitchen? What are you doing *(giggling)* here?
ZANDILE:	I'm reading.
LINDIWE:	You are always reading. What are you reading now? *(Zandile hides the magazine behind her back)*
ZANDILE:	Guess. Just Bona.
LINDIWE:	*(Laughs)* I remember when we used to hide those in our Biology books.
ZANDILE:	History books.
LINDIWE:	Hey listen tshomam, I've got serious news to tell you. My mother told me she received a letter from my aunt and they want me to go to Jo'burg.
ZANDILE:	Jo'burg? The big city.
LINDIWE:	Hey wena, my cousin's getting married and they want me to be a bridesmaid.
ZANDILE:	You are lucky Lindiwe, but I wish you were going to Durban man.
LINDIWE:	Why? Jo'burg is better.
ZANDILE:	You could find my grandmother in Durban.
LINDIWE:	Zandile, how will I know which is your grandmother? I'll have to ask all the grandmothers *(laughs)*. I can't wait to sing those wedding songs. *(They both start singing a wedding song and end up laughing excitedly on the floor)*
ZANDILE:	When are you leaving man?

58

LINDIWE:	Next Saturday, ha ha!
ZANDILE:	Saturday … hawu, Lindi, you are going to miss my performance if you leave on Saturday.
LINDIWE:	What?
ZANDILE:	I'm doing a praise poem for Mr Hlatshwayo, you know he is going on pension.
LINDIWE:	Hawu tshomam, I'm so sorry but ooh, the wedding in JHB.
ZANDILE:	But can't I at least show you my new dress?
LINDIWE:	Yes, let me see the dress. *(Zandile exits to fetch her praise poetry costume)*
LINDIWE:	Ooh, but I'm so excited. I can't wait to get to Johannesburg. *(Zandile re-enters)*
ZANDILE:	I'm so nervous. What do you think? I'm not sure about the colour?
LINDIWE:	*(half interested as Zandile turns round to be seen.)* It's nice, but I hear that Jo'burg is a big city. And I'm taking a train by myself.
ZANDILE:	You are going to enjoy yourself Lindiwe!
LINDIWE:	And there are going to be some …
TOGETHER:	Nice boys!
ZANDILE:	Shhh, keep your voice down!
ZANDILE:	Who's meeting you wena?
LINDIWE:	And I've never been in a train by myself before.
ZANDILE:	You must be careful ne? All those boys from town are dangerous.
LINDIWE:	Hayi! They're putting me in second class. They say it's safe. Hey man, I want you to see me off at the station.
ZANDILE:	I'll ask my mother, but Lindi man, what will Mzwakhe say?

59

LINDIWE:	Hawu, Mzwakhe is just a schoolboy.
ZANDILE:	But he likes you.
LINDIWE:	But I'm going to Jo'burg now, I'm going to meet sophisticated men! Maybe bring one for you?
ZANDILE:	I don't know.
LINDIWE:	Yes!
ZANDILE:	Hayi suka, I've got enough problems with Matshezi's son.
LINDIWE:	Ha! But that one is not getting anywhere!
ZANDILE:	*(Changing subject)* Lindiwe, what time are you leaving on Saturday?
LINDIWE:	At 3 o'clock in the afternoon.
ZANDILE:	And what are you going to wear?
LINDIWE:	I'm going to be wearing my red mini-skirt.
ZANDILE:	Jo, the red one?
LINDIWE:	Yes.
ZANDILE:	My God.
LINDIWE:	My platform shoes and my red beret and I have a new white blouse.
ZANDILE:	Jo! You are going to look beautiful.
LINDIWE:	Yes, red and white.
ZANDILE:	Red and white, ishaft iyasifakazela! *(Laughs)*
LINDIWE:	What are you going to wear to the station?
ZANDILE:	Aaa … I don't know.
LINDIWE:	Don't wear your terylene skirt please.
ZANDILE:	But it's nice, Lindiwe.
LINDIWE:	Terylene skirts are too old fashioned now. It's 1976, you must look sharp!
ZANDILE:	But my mother won't let me wear my other clothes just to go out to the station.

LINDIWE:	You can sneak them out.
ZANDILE:	Yes, I could take them on Friday and hide them at your place.
LINDIWE:	Yes. Then I'll keep them with me and you can just wear your terylene skirt when you come and when you get there you …
TOGETHER:	Change!
ZANDILE:	Lindiwe, ufuna i-orange squash?
LINDIWE:	No, but now I must go, I still have to cook supper and start packing and organise.
ZANDILE:	Awusandiqhosheli. Okay. I'll see you, if not before, Friday night. We are going to look …
TOGETHER:	Sharp!

Blackout!

PRAISE POETRY AND GOGO'S ENTRANCE

Zandile walks into the light as if on to a school stage, dressed in her kaftan. She addresses the audience a little shyly.

ZANDILE: Good afternoon. I feel very honoured to have been chosen to do this praise poem for Mr Hlatshwayo. This is the kind of thing I learned from my grandmother. She was a very good storyteller.

Hlatshwayo, Ngwane, Mhayisa, Ncam Ncam. Mfazindini onamabele amade nang-aphesheya komfula uyamunyisa. Untlamvu azimshayi ziyamthantalaza. Usikhumba sehlula abeshuki. Dondolo lamaNgisi nam-aNkelemane. Mhayisa!

Zandile completes the first part of Mr Hlatshwayo's family praise name, which every African family has. These names outline each family's history. She then starts a song

Mayidibane bafazi balelali. Mayidibane bafunde abantabethu (Let's get together women of this village. Let's get together so our children can learn)

*While Zandile sings this song on one side
of the stage, on the other side the spot-
light shines on Gogo, who comes in with
some presents for Zandile, wrapped in
colourful paper and she thoughtfully
packs them in a suitcase. As she exits, the
song gets louder and Zandile resumes the
poetry. Now she focusses on the praises
of Mr Hlatshwayo himself — what he
has achieved and done for his people*

Mde ngeentonga. Nkcuba buchopho
eyavumbuka emanzini iphethe ulwazi.
Nzulu lwazi eyavumbuka emanzini
iphethe ukuzinikela. Nkunzi ndini
emandla. Wena owagila ngophondo.
Zathi iziphazamiso zaqikileka phantsi.
Zaxela unkunzana ziphethwe ngumben-
deni. Wathi ukugawulela phantsi intsa-
sana emile endleleni yakho. Seva ngo
khenkce! khenkce! Seva ngo khenkce!
khenkce! Seva ngo khenkce! Yathi im-
ikhenkce yasebusika yanyibilika nga-
phantsi kwefutha lenyawo zakho. Kuba
kalokhu wena wawuxhabashele ukuza
kupha thina imfundo. Wawuxhabashele
ukuza kupha thina ukhanyo

Sasisiva sixakeka xa kuthethwa ngem-
fundo. Sasisiva sixhatshelwe zingqondo
xa kuthethwa ngenkqubela phambili.
Suka wena — wawelela ngeneno. Ubuso
bakho bumamatheka.Wabulisa savuma.
Wabalisa samamela.Wafundisa saphula-
phula. Wancokola — tyhini sahleka!

64

Kanti ngokwenze njalo wena uyazi ukuba uyatyala. Nathi namhlanje siya-zidla. Ngenxa yakho siyavuna Mhayisa!

SCENE THIRTEEN

ZANDILE AND LINDIWE PREPARE FOR THE FAREWELL PARTY

Lindiwe comes to visit after the examinations.

LINDIWE: Zandi!

ZANDILE: Yebo.

TOGETHER: We did it! *(Laugh)*

LINDIWE: No more books.

ZANDILE: No more swotting.

LINDIWE: Matric is done forever. What if we don't pass?

ZANDILE: Of course we'll pass, Lindiwe.

LINDIWE: Anyway we can worry about that when the results come out next month.

ZANDILE: But tomorrow ...

TOGETHER: It's a party *(laugh excitedly, and start singing)*. Oh what a night! Hey! Late December 1963. What a very special time for me ... what a lady what a night! *(They collapse with laughter)*

LINDIWE:	I have been waiting for this day!
ZANDILE:	But you are glad you came back, aren't you?
LINDIWE:	Aah, I had no choice ... my parents forced me to come back.
ZANDILE:	They were right, you know, six months wasn't such a long time.
LINDIWE:	It's been too long for me because I want to see my Paul again.
ZANDILE:	Ever since you came back from that wedding, it's just Paul ... Paul ... Paul.
LINDIWE:	Because you don't know what happened to me the first time I saw Paul at the wedding ha!
ZANDILE:	Lindiwe, I have heard this a few million times now, I know your heart stopped and you started sweating just like in the Barbara Cartland books.
LINDIWE:	I can tell you this over and over.
ZANDILE:	Let me tell you what's going to make my heart stop ... I'm worried ... what are we presenting at the party tomorrow?
LINDIWE:	*(Laughs)* Do you remember last year's party?
ZANDILE:	We were attending on last year's matrics. And were they boring!
LINDIWE:	And you ... with the tray!
ZANDILE:	Don't remind me please.
LINDIWE:	You were walking along with the big tray.
ZANDILE:	Yes. There were twenty-four plastic cups filled with Coca-Cola.
LINDIWE:	For the twelve prefects and their partners.
ZANDILE:	I remember the tune that was playing: 'Papa was a Rolling Stone'. As I was walking nicely along to the music with the tray

	then that stupid clumsy Zola danced right into me!
LINDIWE:	Nonsense! You tripped. Those shoes you had on were too tight. Why is it your shoes were always too small for you?
ZANDILE:	This boy danced right into me and over I went, on to the headboy's lap and his girlfriend, I forget her name now ...
LINDIWE:	Caroline.
ZANDILE:	*(Imitating Caroline in Zulu)* 'I always knew you had your eyes on Sipho.'
LINDIWE:	As if you were so desperate.
ZANDILE:	Meanwhile my eyes were on the floor.
LINDIWE:	And there was Coca-Cola everywhere, all over the pretty pink and blue and ...
ZANDILE:	Yellow.
LINDIWE:	Dresses were ruined. I laughed. You! Your face was blushing.
ZANDILE:	Everybody was so sticky and so cross.
LINDIWE:	Ah, but at least it woke them up.
ZANDILE:	Let's stop laughing at other people. What are we going to do tomorrow?
LINDIWE:	Maybe we can do a song Paul taught me.
ZANDILE:	Paul again. Lindiwe, this Paul is haunting us now. Who invented telephones? Paul. Who discovered the sea route to India? Paul ... Paul *(mocking)*.
LINDIWE:	You are jealous.
ZANDILE:	Okay, let's do his song. What is it?
LINDIWE:	'Sugar Sugar'.
ZANDILE:	Does that mean I'm going to be your sugar sugar tomorrow? *(Laughs)*
LINDIWE:	Haai suka wena! *(She starts singing and dancing)* Sugar Sugar ...
ZANDILE:	And what do I sing?

LINDIWE:	Pa pum pa pum ...
ZANDILE:	Pa pum pa pum ... Okay let's try.
LINDIWE:	Sugar Sugar ...
ZANDILE:	Pa pum pa pum ...
LINDIWE:	Oh, honey honey ...
ZANDILE:	Pa pa pum ... *(Lindiwe stares at the way Zandile is dancing and stops singing in horror)*
LINDIWE:	You can't dance like this. Oh, they will laugh at you — you must shake like this! *She shows Zandile)*
ZANDILE:	Well, you must teach me Lindiwe.
LINDIWE:	Sugar Sugar ... *(shaking)*
ZANDILE:	Pa pum pa pum ...
LINDIWE:	Oh honey honey ...
ZANDILE:	Pa pum pa pum ...
LINDIWE:	*(Stops again)* Zandile ... haai haai ... your shoulders! Ezase Jo'burg!
ZANDILE:	Alright — siyafunda eJo'burg!
LINDIWE:	Sugar Sugar ...
ZANDILE:	Pa pum pa pum ...
LINDIWE:	Oh, honey honey ...
ZANDILE:	Pa pum pa pum ...
LINDIWE:	Your knees ... go down! Sugar Sugar ...
ZANDILE:	Pa pum pa pum ...
LINDIWE:	Your knees ... Sugar Sugar ...
ZANDILE:	Pa pum pa pum ...
LINDIWE:	Oh, honey honey ... *(Zandile is concentrating on her knees and forgets to sing)*
LINDIWE:	And sing at the same time! You are my candy girl ...
ZANDILE:	Hey?
TOGETHER:	And you got me wanting you! *(They laugh and exclaim in Xhosa: "We'll show them.")*
ZANDILE:	I like this, but is this all your Paul does? He doesn't work he just sings

	sugar sugar to you all day long? That's marriage material.
LINDIWE:	Suka! He does work.
ZANDILE:	What does he do?
LINDIWE:	He plays drums.
ZANDILE:	You call that work?
LINDIWE:	It's hard work drumming.
ZANDILE:	What does his family say, a grown-up man playing drums? *(She imitates a drummer)*
LINDIWE:	They like it. His sisters always come to watch him, Thandi and Phumzile.
ZANDILE:	Are they our age?
LINDIWE:	No, they are old, about 27 and 28 and they like me!
ZANDILE:	Did you see his parents?
LINDIWE:	No, the parents are in Durban, but Paul says he has already told them about me.
ZANDILE:	Mmmm! It looks quite serious Lindiwe.
LINDIWE:	Yes. Mrs Zwide anyday now!
ZANDILE:	Zwide?
LINDIWE:	Yes.
ZANDILE:	You say Paul has two sisters Thandi and Phumzile? And that they are older than him and that the family is in Durban and that their surname is Zwide? Please give me your Paul's address.
LINDIWE:	But why?
ZANDILE:	Because I need to write to him. It's very important.
LINDIWE:	But what's the connection? *(Stands up, getting suspicious and jealous)*
ZANDILE:	Because Zwide, that's my family name.
LINDIWE:	Sigwili?
ZANDILE:	Is my mother's name. Zandile Zwide is my real name. Zwide is my father's name.

LINDIWE:	Zandi, are you trying to tell me that Paul might be your brother?
ZANDILE:	He could be my half brother from Durban. Your Paul plays drums? I remember I was about seven years old, my half brother in Durban, Paul, used to take the old cake tins, put them down, play drums with them, and my father could never stop him. And the sisters' names connect with my half sisters in Durban. I want to know where my grandmother is.
LINDIWE:	Gogo *(thinks)*. Zandile, there is an old woman living there where Paul stays with his uncle. It could be your grandmother.
ZANDILE:	Oh, Gogo. Nkosi yami!
LINDIWE:	Let me go now. I will run home to get Paul's number and then go straight to the Post Office to phone him.
ZANDILE:	Lindiwe, I am coming with you.
LINDIWE:	No, I'm phoning Paul at work. Even if it is your grandmother you won't talk to her!
ZANDILE:	Lindiwe, just run and come straight back, Okay?
LINDIWE:	For sure, Sister-in-law!
ZANDILE:	Oh God let it be him, let it be the right Paul and ... so I can see Gogo. Please God don't let anything happen to her. Where is Lindiwe? Please, please. I want to go and stay with her again. It will be so nice to stay with her. My own grandmother. Now I can do things for her. I can cook for her, like she used to cook for me. Shame she must be old now. I will cook amadombolo, bake nice cakes for her. Where is Lindwe? ... Make tea for her and bring it to her bed. Every

morning — oh I wish I could fly! *(She becomes impatient and moves towards the passage in pursuit of Lindi)* Lindi, Lindiwe, where are you? Come on now, Lindiwe. I want to know. *(She exits end of passage)*

SCENE FOURTEEN

ZANDILE FINDS GOGO'S SUITCASE

An old woman enters carrying a Bible and leaning on a walking stick

ZANDILE: Nkqo! Nkqo! Nkqo! *(Zandile is knocking offstage)*

OLD WOMAN: Ubani? Who is it?

ZANDILE: Yimina uZandile. Gogo sengibuyile. I've come back.

OLD WOMAN: Ngena. *(Zandile enters and sees the old woman and for a split second thinks it's her grandmother)*

ZANDILE: Gogo, yimina uZandile. *(She stops)* Sanibonani.

OLD WOMAN: Sawubona Zandile.

ZANDILE: Is my grandmother here?

OLD WOMAN: Hlala phansi Mntanomntanami. You don't know me but you know uncle Phillip's wife — I'm her mother.

ZANDILE: Has Gogo gone to fetch me from the station?

OLD WOMAN: No Mntanomntanami — she has left us.

ZANDILE:	Has she gone ... has she moved?
OLD WOMAN:	No, no – she always knew you would come back. She told me so many stories about you. Oh, she wanted to see you ... right until the end she was asking for you.
ZANDILE:	But where is she?
OLD WOMAN:	Oh, Mntanomntanami ... she passed away.
ZANDILE:	Aw, no, not my grandmother.
OLD WOMAN:	I'm so sorry. UGogo Mthwalo, she was visiting here with us when she got sick. We were great friends. Uncle Phillip organised doctors. They did everything they could. We did our best to make her comfortable.
ZANDILE:	I wish I could have been here.
OLD WOMAN:	Zandile, it was her time to go.
ZANDILE:	Did she ever know what happened to me, that I went to the Transkei?
OLD WOMAN:	Yes, and she knew that your mother took you and that it was not your will to go.
ZANDILE:	But why didn't she come and fetch me? I waited for her.
OLD WOMAN:	She did try but they would never tell her exactly where you were.
ZANDILE:	I wish she had waited for me.
OLD WOMAN:	She must have known you'd find her. She said to me – if ever my child comes back or if they trace her, give her this photo. *(She takes a photograph out of her Bible)* And she left a suitcase for you. She said I must give it to you. *(She goes to fetch it)*
ZANDILE:	Oh, uGogo nkosi yami!

OLD WOMAN: She would have been proud to see you, so tall and beautiful. How old are you now Mntanomntanami?

ZANDILE: Eighteen.

OLD WOMAN: Eighteen!

ZANDILE: Did she say I must take the suitcase?

OLD WOMAN: *(Nods)* She said it was yours, and she asked me to give you the key ... here. I will leave you now. *(Exits)*

Zandile is on her own in a pool of light, very quiet, very separated from her surroundings. She opens the suitcase and takes out all the little parcels her grandmother has been putting away for her through all the years. Zandile holds each of them for a moment, before laying them gently to one side. At the bottom of the suitcase she finds a dress, takes it out and holds it up against herself. It is a little girl's dress, which barely reaches beyond her waist. She puts it down, reaches for a second dress and repeats the action. She picks up a third dress and also holds it against her body. She then holds all three dresses closely to her, hugging them and sobbing. The lights slowly fade to black ...

TRANSLATIONS

Many of the phrases in *Have You Seen Zandile?* need no translation; they are made clear by the context, or are given in English immediately after the Zulu or Xhosa phrase.

The following words appear repeatedly in the play and are simply translated:

> Gogo – Grandmother
> Mntanomntanami – Grandchild
> wena – you, hey you
> Sawubona – Hello

Longer passages, or short phrases that are not clear in context, are given in translation below. Indications are given by scene number and page number. Where necessary for the sake of clarity, English language cues are given in italics.

SCENE ONE

page 1, lines 1 – 11

ZANDILE: Did you see how that small boy was given a good hiding as he was trying to be smart again? He got it on the rear end – whack, whack! He ran away. The other children laughed at him. Goodbye, I'll see you tomorrow. Hey, Nomusa, remember to bring the skipping rope – I'll bring crayons ... Nomusa, you promised – don't make a fool of me ... bye bye ... bye bye.

page 2, lines 1 – 5

ZANDILE: There are our mothers, carrying parcels
There are our mothers, carrying loads
Mmmm, Mmmmm, there are our mothers
We see rice, we see meat
We see cakes, we see sweets

lines 17 – 18

ZANDILE: Pooh! I'm making a fool of myself. I don't have any sweet here, *it's just a stone!*

page 3, line 9

ZANDILE: My name is Zandile ...

page 4, line 3
ZANDILE: *… you so much.* Never!
line 24
ZANDILE: *… don't stand on tip toe,* you're cheating,
line 31
ZANDILE: *… this (demonstrates)* with such style…
page 5, lines 3 – 4
ZANDILE: *… can put rouge on your lips* like this white lady, Mrs. Webber …
lines 5 – 10
ZANDILE: *And Bongi, we can speak English –* and I can say, What's the matter with you? *(Stops and thinks) Bongi, you can also have a car!* Then you can give me a lift, and we can ride together, beautifully dressed, and people would admire us and say, wow, baby!

SCENE TWO

page 7, lines 1 – 2
GOGO: Hello, MaGumede! (Laughs) How are you? We are well.

SCENE THREE

page 11, line 1
ZANDILE: I enjoyed being in town, Gogo, *and I* …
lines 4 – 9
ZANDILE: And I also enjoyed such big bananas, *I like banana, and Gogo, do you remember when we got a lift* in the rickshaw? *I thought I was going to fall at the back when he started to run with us.* Gogo, aren't you afraid of the rickshaw's loud horn?
page 12, line 1
ZANDILE: What can I have to drink, Gogo?
line 28
ZANDILE: Gogo, can we have cakes?
page 13, lines 5 – 6
ZANDILE: *… 'Happy Family')* Isn't this you and me on the biscuit tin?
line 14
GOGO: Let me see your books now.

lines 17 – 20
ZANDILE: We did arithmetic, and I got ten out of ten.
I'll go fetch my book and show you.
See, *I got correct ...*

lines 25 – 27
ZANDILE: *I played this game:* 'As I was walking along,
walking along'. Every time I pause, Gogo,
you must say, 'Two Shillings'. All right, let's
start.

line 31
ZANDILE: I met two young men.

line 32
GOGO: Three Shillings.

page 14, lines 1 – 2
ZANDILE: No, no. Gogo. It's Two Shillings, every time.

line 3
GOGO: Oh, I see. Every time?

line 9
ZANDILE: They stopped to greet me.

line 11
ZANDILE: They asked me my name.

line 13
ZANDILE: I told them that I am Zandile.

line 15
ZANDILE: They asked me where I belonged.

lines 17 – 19
ZANDILE: I told them I am of the Mthembu of Qhu-
deni's, Mvelase of Mpofane clan, the one
who crossed the Thukela River because of
starvation.

line 24
ZANDILE: They asked me if I had a boyfriend.

lines 26 – 27
ZANDILE: I told them I don't have a boyfriend, I'm still
a schoolgirl, a schoolgirl, a mere schoolgirl!

line 32
ZANDILE: *... going to be good.* Isn't that right, Gogo?

page 15, line 15
ZANDILE: On mine it says, 'Big Ears'.

line 18
GOGO: Gracious, no no no …

line 23
ZANDILE: I am the love of your heart, aren't I, Gogo?

page 18, lines 3 – 4
GOGO: *(She starts the prayer while tidying up)* Yes, The Lord is my shepherd …

line 7
GOGO: I shall not want …

line 9
GOGO: He makes me lie down in green pastures …

SCENE FOUR (a)

page 21, lines 30 – 34
ZANDILE: Farewell, Vuyelwa
Don't disgrace us to our in-laws
God bless
God shower his blessings
Farewell, Vuyelwa

SCENE FOUR (b)

page 23, line 18
ZANDILE: No. I don't want to. *(I've been teaching them …*

page 24, lines 2 – 3
GOGO: *… song. (She starts singing)* Get up, get up, Zola, we're here –

lines 10 – 17
GOGO: Get up – get up – Zola – We are here – Ah – are you sleeping? – Are you sleeping? *(Zandile joins in on the odd words when she feels confident with a note or word)* We'll take a bus – Zola – to Durban – Ah – Are you sleeping? Are you sleeping? We'll see the sea and the waves – Zola. Ah – Are you sleeping? Are you sleeping?

Page 26, lines 11 – 13
GOGO: *… with a new broom –* (ululating and boasting to a woman with no children)

SCENE FIVE

page 27, lines 1 – 9

ZANDILE: Congratulations
Congratulations!
Zandile has passed!
She will be going to Port Shepstone with
Gogo.

SCENE SIX

page 29, lines 3 – 5

GOGO: Ntombizandile! Your grandmother uMthwalo
Uboshiwe is back. We are leaving today, ...*we
are going to Port* ...

SCENE EIGHT

page 38, line 7

LULAMA: Don't be silly! *(Zandile gets up as if to leave the
...*

line 10

LULAMA: How odd! *I didn't say go and wash.*

SCENE NINE

page 43, lines 1 - 5

ZANDILE: Hurray! I got here first! *(She turns as if she
expects to see Lindiwe behind her. There is no
Lindiwe)* Come quickly, Lindi. You tall one
just like somebody I love!

lines 11 – 12

ZANDILE: *water,* as if saying, 'I'm beautiful this side,
I'm ugly on this side. This is the part that
makes me beautiful'.

page 44, line 7

ZANDILE: A snake! A snake!

line 13

LINDIWE: You're such a coward. What snake?

line 29

ZANDILE: ... *legs. She told us* a water snake *bit her.*

line 30

LINDIWE: You know what, Zandile?

page 45, line 8

LINDIWE: Oh, God, I don't even want to think about it.

lines 15 – 16
ZANDILE: *You can't! It's rude,* what's the matter with you?

line 25
ZANDILE: *They make babies* at the hospital?

page 46, lines 22 – 23
LINDIWE: … *what they say about a man* – 'that he is judged by his cattle, not by his good looks'.

page 47, line 12
ZANDILE: She looks as beautiful as the morning star.

line 20
LINDIWE: Zandile! Cracks on your feet?

page 48, line 3
ZANDILE: … *than mine*. You already have big breasts.

page 61, line 8
ZANDILE: Lindiwe, do you want an orange squash?

line 11
ZANDILE: You're boasting.

SCENE TWELVE

pages 63 – 65
ZANDILE: … *She was a very good storyteller.*
First I would like to say, Greetings to our
principal on behalf of my fellow students.
Greetings to the son of Hlatshwayo
Hlatshwayo, son of Mhayisa
Mhayisa the son of Ngwane
Ngwane the bravest chief this side of the river
Thukela!
…
The time has come for you to sit down and
   relax
Stretch out those tired legs
And listen to the song of praise
Coming from happy young voices
They sing of a short little man
Who had drunk from the well of knowledge
And so wanted to share it with his people
He armed himself with a matchett
Ready to fell any obstacles that stood in
   his way

And for a while, the sound of his matchett
    was all people could hear
Khenkce! Khenkce!
Seva ngo Khenkce! Khenkce!
Seva ngo Khenkce! Khenkce!
Seva ngo Khenkce! A matchett hard at work.

A school – that was his plan
A fountain of knowledge was what he had
    in mind
A fireplace to cook great minds!
For he had heard the call from across the
    big river
He had heard the bird calls from deep in
    the forest
And he asked himself
Were the ancestors speaking to him
through the sweet melodious bird calls?
Did the ancestors want him to stand up on
    a rock
And be seen by all the young knowledge-
    seekers?
Brave man that he was
He answered the call
He spent his life planting seeds
In our hearts and our minds

And today – we are a proud people
From today till the end of time
All the young and old voices
Will shout out loud, to the most deserving
    man
In this village
Camagu! Hlatshwayo, we thank you
Camagu! Mhayisa, we salute you
Camagu!

SCENE FOURTEEN
page 75, line 4
ZANDILE: It's Zandile, Gogo. I've come back.
line 13
OLD WOMAN: Sit down, Zandile.